LE CORDON BLEU

HOME COLLECTION

·SALADS·

MEREHURST

contents

4
Artichoke and baby spinach salad

6
Caesar salad

8
Golden carrot and cardamom salad

10
Fattoush

12
Celery à la portugaise

14
*Chargrilled vegetables with
balsamic vinegar dressing*

16
Nutty chicken liver salad

18
*Prawn pasta salad with
tarragon pesto*

20
Coleslaw

22
Caprese/Cucumber yoghurt and dill

24
*Goat's cheese with a watercress and
lamb's lettuce salad*

26
Wild rice and haloumi salad

28
Kaleidoscope salad

30
Lentil and bacon salad

32
Mixed salad/Lorette salad

34
*Smoked trout salad with
horseradish sauce*

36
Mixed beans in sweet and sour tomato

38
Waldorf salad

40
Salmon salade niçoise

42
Oriental lime chicken salad

44
*Classic potato salad/Mustard seed
potato salad*

46
Celeriac remoulade

48
Melon and seafood sesame salad

50
Tabouleh/Rustic Greek salad

52
Seared scallop and mango salsa salad

54
*Smoked chicken salad with a
macadamia nut dressing*

56
Warm fennel and cherry tomato salad

58
Thai pork salad

60
Three-tomato salad

62
Duck salad with plum dressing

recipe ratings ❁ *easy* ❁❁ *a little more care needed* ❁❁❁ *more care needed*

Artichoke and baby spinach salad

An attractive salad of summery green colours, textures and flavours with the crunch of toasted pumpkin seeds and a creamy avocado dressing.

*Preparation time **35 minutes***
*Total cooking time **35 minutes***
Serves 4

6 large globe artichokes
juice of 1 lemon
45 g (1 1/2 oz) pumpkin seeds
250 g (8 oz) baby spinach
2 teaspoons extra virgin olive oil

DRESSING
1 ripe avocado
juice of 1–2 limes
1 clove garlic
2 tablespoons extra virgin olive oil or cream

1 Break off each artichoke stalk, pulling out the fibres that attach it to the base. Pull off the outer leaves and place the artichokes in a pan of salted water with the lemon juice. Weigh down with a plate, bring to the boil and simmer for 20–35 minutes, testing for doneness by pulling at one of the leaves. If it comes away easily, the artichoke is done. Pull off the remaining leaves (you can eat the artichoke leaves separately, dipped in vinaigrette, or just eat them as you pull them off) and remove the hairy choke in the middle of the artichoke with a teaspoon, then discard. Cut the bases into quarters and place in water, to which a little extra lemon juice has been added, while you prepare the rest of the salad.

2 Preheat a grill to medium. Toast the pumpkin seeds by placing on a baking tray and grilling for 1–2 minutes, turning once or twice and taking care not to let the seeds burn.

3 To make the dressing, cut the avocado in half, remove the stone and peel off the skin. Cut the flesh into chunks and place in a blender with half the lime juice, the garlic and some salt and black pepper. Blend the mixture until smooth, add the olive oil or cream and blend for another few seconds to incorporate. Thin the dressing slightly if required with the remaining lime juice or olive oil.

4 Wash the baby spinach thoroughly in several changes of water and drain well before placing in a bowl. Drizzle a little extra olive oil over the leaves, season with salt and black pepper and toss to evenly coat. Place the spinach in the centre of four plates and arrange the drained artichoke pieces around them. Drizzle the dressing around the edge and sprinkle with the toasted pumpkin seeds.

Caesar salad

This salad is often thought of as an American dish, but it was actually created by Caesar Cardini in Tijuana, Mexico, in the 1920s. This main-course version is served with Parmesan crisps.

*Preparation time **25 minutes***
*Total cooking time **25 minutes***
Serves 4

PARMESAN CRISPS
200 g (6¹/2 oz) Parmesan, finely grated
¹/2 teaspoon brown mustard seeds

DRESSING
2 small cloves garlic, crushed
2 egg yolks
90 ml (3 fl oz) olive oil
1 teaspoon Worcestershire sauce
1 tablespoon lemon juice
55 g (1³/4 oz) Parmesan, finely grated

3 baby cos or 4 little gem lettuces
8 slices white bread
6 tablespoons olive oil or unsalted butter
90 g (3 oz) anchovy fillets, chopped

1 Preheat the oven to moderate 180°C (350°F/Gas 4).
2 To make the Parmesan crisps, line a baking tray with baking paper. Using a quarter of the Parmesan, sprinkle two long, thin triangular shapes onto the prepared tray. Sprinkle with black pepper and a quarter of the mustard seeds and bake for 4–5 minutes, or until the cheese has melted and is a light golden colour. Remove from the oven and leave to cool and harden. Once cooled, slide carefully off the tray and repeat with the remaining Parmesan, mustard seeds and some black pepper until you have made eight Parmesan triangles.

3 To make the dressing, whisk the garlic and egg yolks together in a large bowl, then add the olive oil, drop-by-drop to begin with, then in a thin, steady stream, whisking continuously until the dressing starts to thicken. Add the Worcestershire sauce, lemon juice and Parmesan and whisk to blend.

4 Separate the lettuce leaves, cut into bite-sized pieces and place in a large bowl. Remove the crusts from the slices of bread and cut into 1 cm (¹/2 inch) cubes. Heat the olive oil or butter in a frying pan and fry the bread until crisp and golden brown. Add to the bowl and mix together with half the dressing. Arrange the dressed salad leaves on four plates, scatter over the anchovy, drizzle a little extra dressing around and decorate with the Parmesan crisps and some black pepper.

Golden carrot and cardamom salad

Who would have thought that a carrot salad could be so unusual? Carrot is combined here with cardamom pods, saffron, orange juice and sultanas to give a distinctly Eastern flavour.

*Preparation time **20 minutes + 2 hours 30 minutes infusing + optional 3–4 days marinating***
*Total cooking time **5 minutes***
*Serves **4–6***

60 ml (2 fl oz) peanut oil
8 cardamom pods, crushed
125 g (4 oz) golden sultanas
3 pinches of saffron threads
4 tablespoons orange juice
125 g (4 oz) unsalted peanuts
750 g (1 1/2 lb) carrots, peeled and grated
juice of 1/2 lemon

1 Three or four days before serving the salad, place the oil into a small pan with the cardamom pods and heat until just warm. Transfer to a clean preserving or jam jar and leave in the refrigerator for 3–4 days to allow the flavours to develop. If time is short, do this just before preparing the rest of the salad. The flavour will be good, just less developed.

2 On the day of serving, place the sultanas, saffron threads and orange juice into a small pan and bring to just below boiling point over a medium heat. Remove from the heat and set aside to infuse for 30 minutes.

3 Have ready a slotted spoon and some paper towels for draining, then heat the cardamom oil in a frying pan, add the peanuts and fry for about 45 seconds, or until just beginning to turn golden brown. Remove the peanuts from the oil with the slotted spoon and drain on the paper towels. Discard the cardamom pods and reserve the remaining oil.

4 Place the carrot in a large bowl and mix in the cardamom-flavoured oil, sultanas and soaking liquid. Season with salt and black pepper and stir in the peanuts and lemon juice. If possible, cover the salad and leave for two hours before serving.

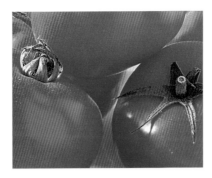

Fattoush

This Middle Eastern salad is traditionally garnished with toasted Arab or Lebanese bread and is brightly flavoured with fresh mint and parsley.

*Preparation time **40 minutes***
*Total cooking time **5 minutes***
Serves 4

4 ripe tomatoes
1 small cos or romaine lettuce
1 small cucumber
1 green capsicum (pepper)
2 French shallots, finely chopped
4 spring onions, finely sliced
4 tablespoons fresh mint, finely chopped
4 tablespoons fresh flat-leaf parsley, finely chopped
2 pitta breads or other similar flat breads

DRESSING
1 clove garlic
1 teaspoon salt
60 ml (2 fl oz) lemon juice
125 ml (4 fl oz) olive oil
few drops of Tabasco sauce

1 Bring a small pan of water to the boil. With the point of a small sharp knife, score a small cross in the skin at the base of the tomatoes. Drop the tomatoes into the boiling water for 10 seconds, then plunge into a bowl of cold water. Peel the skin away from the cross, then cut around and remove the stalk from the tomatoes. Slice the tomatoes into quarters, remove and discard the seeds and finely dice the flesh. Place in a bowl.

2 Shred the lettuce into 1 cm ($^1/_2$ inch) strips and add to the tomato. Peel the cucumber, slice it into quarters lengthways and remove the seeds with a teaspoon. Cut the flesh into cubes and place in the bowl. Cut the capsicum into similar sized cubes. Add to the bowl with the shallots, spring onion, mint and parsley. Stir the salad gently to combine.

3 To make the dressing, crush the garlic and mix with the salt to form a paste. Use a fork to whisk the lemon juice, olive oil and Tabasco into the garlic, then season with black pepper to taste.

4 Finally, toast the pitta bread on both sides until it is golden brown and crisp. Using a sharp knife, cut the bread into 1 cm ($^1/_2$ inch) squares and add to the salad. Pour in the dressing, toss together until evenly combined and serve immediately. This salad is wonderful with grilled meats and kebabs.

Celery à la portugaise

A warm salad that can be a wonderful accompaniment to a main meal, a colourful buffet dish or, when served with Portuguese bread rolls, a vegetarian meal in its own right.

*Preparation time **25 minutes***
*Total cooking time **55 minutes***

Serves 4

500–600 g (1–1 1/4 lb) celery hearts
800 g (1 lb 10 oz) ripe tomatoes
2 tablespoons olive oil
1 onion, finely chopped
2 cloves garlic, chopped
1 tablespoon tomato paste
105 ml (3 1/2 fl oz) white wine
1 bouquet garni
16 whole black olives
2 tablespoons fresh parsley, chopped

1 Using a sharp knife, cut through the core of each celery heart to make quarters, making sure the stems stay joined at the base. If they are too large to sit on a plate attractively, cut the length down to about 18 cm (7 inches). Bring a large pan of salted water to the boil and, once boiling, cook the celery for 1 minute. Remove using a slotted spoon and rinse under cold water until completely cold. Keep the pan of water simmering gently on the stove.

2 With the point of a small sharp knife, score a small cross in the skin at the base of the tomatoes. Drop the tomatoes into the boiling water for 10 seconds, then plunge them into a bowl of cold water. Peel the skin away from the cross, then cut around and remove the stalk from the tomatoes. Slice the tomatoes into quarters and remove and discard the seeds. Finely dice the flesh and place in a bowl.

3 In a heavy-based pan, heat the oil and gently fry the onion and garlic for 5–10 minutes, or until they begin to soften but are not coloured. Add the tomato with the tomato paste, wine, bouquet garni and 300 ml (10 fl oz) water. Season well with salt and black pepper, then add the celery hearts and simmer for 30–40 minutes, or until the celery is tender. Remove the bouquet garni and serve the salad warm, garnished with the black olives and parsley.

Chargrilled vegetables with balsamic vinegar dressing

In this beautiful dish, the vegetables are seared to add colour and the quick cooking time means they retain their crispness and flavour.

*Preparation time **10 minutes***
*Total cooking time **25 minutes***
Serves 4

6 baby or I large eggplant (aubergine)
2 zucchini (courgettes)
I red capsicum (pepper)
I yellow capsicum (pepper)
I green capsicum (pepper)
I tablespoon olive oil
125 g (4 oz) baby sweetcorn

DRESSING
I teaspoon cumin seeds
2 teaspoons honey
2 tablespoons balsamic vinegar
I tablespoon walnut oil
2 tablespoons olive oil

1   Cut the baby eggplants in half lengthways or slice the large eggplant, then diagonally slice the zucchini. Cut the red, yellow and green capsicums in half and remove the seeds, stalk and membrane. Depending on the size of the capsicums, they can be cut again into two or three large pieces.

2   Heat a chargrill pan until it is very hot. Lightly brush with the olive oil, place the eggplant and zucchini on the pan and cook for about 4–6 minutes each side, turning once only, until the vegetables have distinct sear marks on them from the pan and are cooked through. Alternatively, the vegetables can be placed under a preheated grill, but then they will not have the attractive charred lines. Remove the cooked eggplant and zucchini to a plate and brush the pan with a little more oil if necessary. Place the capsicum and baby sweetcorn on the hot pan and cook for 4–5 minutes each side, or until they are cooked through, turning once. Remove to the plate with the other vegetables.

3   To make the dressing, heat a frying pan and dry-roast the cumin seeds for 2 minutes over medium heat, or until barely coloured and releasing their aroma, but taking care not to let them burn. Place the cumin seeds in a small bowl with the honey, balsamic vinegar and oils. Using a small balloon whisk, whisk the dressing briskly and season well with salt and black pepper. Arrange the warm vegetables on a serving plate with the dressing drizzled over and serve with some bread.

Nutty chicken liver salad

A perfectly balanced and unusual combination of sweet chicken livers and tart apples with a creamy, hazelnut-studded sauce.

Preparation time **15 minutes**
Total cooking time **20 minutes**
Serves 4

DRESSING
90 g (3 oz) hazelnuts
220 ml (7 fl oz) natural yoghurt
4 tablespoons dry cider
2 tablespoons snipped fresh chives

2 Granny Smith apples
juice of 1/2 lemon
500 g (1 lb) chicken livers
30 g (1 oz) unsalted butter
1 tablespoon hazelnut oil
4 sprigs of fresh rosemary
3 tablespoons cider vinegar
125 g (4 oz) frisée lettuce
60 g (2 oz) rocket leaves

1 To make the dressing, preheat a grill to medium and toast the hazelnuts for 5 minutes, or until golden. If they are still in their skins, rub these off with a tea towel, then chop quite finely. Allow to cool. Place the yoghurt, cider, chives and some salt and black pepper in a bowl and combine. Cover with plastic film and refrigerate.

2 Core the apples and cut into eight wedges, then cut each piece again into three pieces. Sprinkle with the lemon juice and set aside.

3 Halve the chicken livers, trim off any discoloured areas, dry on paper towels and season lightly with salt and black pepper. In a heavy-based frying pan, heat the butter, oil and rosemary over medium heat, then add the livers and fry for about 6–10 minutes, or until cooked through and very slightly pink in the centre. Remove from the pan and keep warm.

4 Add the cider vinegar to the pan, followed by the apple pieces. Raise the heat to high and cook for about 2–3 minutes, or until the apples are just tender. Remove the apples from the pan and keep warm. Return the livers to the pan and coat with the remaining juices.

5 Tear the frisée and rocket leaves into bite-sized pieces and place in a bowl with the apple. Add the hazelnuts to the dressing and give it a quick stir, then pour a quarter of it into the bowl, tossing to coat the leaves but being careful not to break up the apple. Pile into the centre of four plates, arrange the chicken livers on top and pour over any juices. Thin the remaining dressing to a drizzling consistency by adding a tablespoon of water if necessary, and drizzle around the plate. Serve immediately.

Prawn pasta salad with tarragon pesto

A deliciously fresh-tasting main course that can be served with chunks of hot plain or garlic bread and chilled white wine.

Preparation time **25 minutes**
Total cooking time **15 minutes**
Serves 4

TARRAGON PESTO
60 g (2 oz) fresh parsley, chopped
15 g (1/2 oz) fresh tarragon leaves, chopped
100 g (31/4 oz) Parmesan, grated
2 cloves garlic, roughly chopped
55 g (13/4 oz) blanched almonds, chopped
250 ml (8 fl oz) olive oil

250 g (8 oz) pasta shells
12 raw tiger prawns
grated rind and juice of 1/2 lemon
250 ml (8 fl oz) crème fraîche or sour cream
155 g (5 oz) baby spinach, coarsely shredded

1 To make the tarragon pesto, place the parsley, tarragon, Parmesan, garlic and almonds in a blender or food processor and blend until the mixture resembles coarse breadcrumbs. Season well with salt and black pepper. With the machine running, add the oil in a thin, steady stream until the pesto is the same consistency as thick pouring cream. Place the pesto in the refrigerator.

2 Bring a large pan of salted water to the boil. Add a splash of oil to stop the pasta sticking and cook the shells according to the manufacturer's instructions.

3 Meanwhile, preheat the grill to high, peel and devein the prawns and brush with a little olive oil. Grill for about 4–5 minutes, or until just cooked through. Toss the cooked prawns in half the lemon rind and juice and keep warm.

4 Drain the pasta well and, while still warm, put in a large bowl with the crème fraîche, remaining lemon rind and juice and the baby spinach. Stir in 4 tablespoons of the pesto, a generous seasoning of salt and black pepper and combine well. Arrange the pasta on four plates, top with the prawns and drizzle a little extra pesto over the salad. Serve warm or at room temperature.

Chef's tip Any leftover pesto can be stored in a clean preserving or jam jar in the refrigerator for up to 3 days. Cover the surface completely with a layer of oil to stop the pesto discolouring.

Coleslaw

Once-upon-a-time, before coleslaw was made by supermarkets and sold in plastic tubs…coleslaw the way it used to be.

*Preparation time **30 minutes***
*Total cooking time **Nil***
Serves 6–8

MAYONNAISE
2 egg yolks
I heaped tablespoon Dijon mustard
** or I heaped teaspoon dried mustard powder**
275 ml (9 fl oz) lightly flavoured vegetable oil
I tablespoon white wine vinegar

¹/2 white cabbage
I onion
2 carrots

1 To make the mayonnaise, bring all the ingredients to room temperature and set a large bowl on a damp tea towel to prevent it from moving. Add the egg yolks, mustard, some ground white pepper and a pinch of salt, and mix well with a balloon whisk or electric beaters.
2 Put the oil in a jug that is easy to pour from. While whisking constantly by hand or with electric beaters, pour a steady thin stream of oil into the mixture. Begin with a small amount and stop pouring periodically to allow each addition to emulsify to a thick, creamy mixture. Continue until 100 ml (3¹/4 fl oz) of the oil has been added and the mayonnaise has begun to thicken.
3 Add the vinegar to make the texture slightly thinner. Continue gradually adding the oil and adjust the flavour by adding more vinegar, salt and white pepper if necessary. Add 1–2 tablespoons of boiling water if it curdles or separates.
4 Finely slice the cabbage and onion and coarsely grate the carrot. Place these in a large bowl and mix together gently with your hands. Using your hands or a large metal spoon (the former is a little messy, but gentler and more effective) mix in enough mayonnaise to coat the vegetables. Season to taste and serve.

Chef's tips Up to half the light vegetable oil can be replaced with olive oil, but the flavour of olive oil is too strong to use alone.
 Any unused mayonnaise can be covered tightly and stored in a clean preserving or jam jar in the refrigerator for up to three days.

Caprese

This lovely combination of tomato, mozzarella and basil is an Italian classic. Balsamic vinegar and good olive oil make up the dressing.

Preparation time **15 minutes**
Total cooking time **Nil**
Serves 4 as an accompaniment

4–6 large ripe, full-flavoured tomatoes
300 g (10 oz) fresh mozzarella or bocconcini
1 tablespoon olive oil
2 tablespoons balsamic vinegar
10 g (¹/4 oz) fresh basil leaves

1 Cut the tomatoes horizontally into thin slices and slice the mozzarella to a similar thickness. Sprinkle the base of a serving plate with salt and black pepper, then arrange the tomato and mozzarella in slightly overlapping circles on the plate.
2 Drizzle with the olive oil and balsamic vinegar and sprinkle over the basil leaves, tearing any large leaves with your fingers. Season with salt and black pepper. The salad can be served immediately or covered and set aside at room temperature for several hours, which will allow the flavours to infuse. If you wish to do this, drizzle only half the olive oil and balsamic vinegar over, then drizzle over the remainder just before serving.

Chef's tip Choose tomatoes of any type, just as long as they have some flavour—vine-ripened tomatoes are best. Take a deep sniff before you buy—they should remind you of summer.

Cucumber yoghurt and dill

A refreshing accompaniment or dip that goes particularly well with spicy food and bread.

Preparation time **10 minutes + 30 minutes standing**
Total cooking time **Nil**
Serves 4–6 as an accompaniment

2 telegraph cucumbers
4 teaspoons salt
40 g (1¹/4 oz) fresh dill, finely chopped
400 g (12³/4 oz) natural Greek-style yoghurt

1 Peel the cucumbers and cut in half lengthways. Using a teaspoon, scoop out all of the seeds and slice across the cucumber to make 5 mm (¹/4 inch) crescent shapes.
2 Place the cucumber in a colander, sprinkle with salt and set aside for 30 minutes. Rinse the salt off the cucumber, drain and dry thoroughly on paper towels.
3 Mix the dill with the yoghurt in a bowl. Season to taste with salt and black pepper and stir in the cucumber. Serve within 1 hour with grilled pita bread.

Chef's tip If the mixture splits on standing, give it a stir just before serving to mix it back together again.

Goat's cheese with a watercress and lamb's lettuce salad

The bitter watercress, tangy goat's cheese and home-made herb olive oil marry beautifully to make a simple salad that is ideal to serve as a light meal with fresh bread.

Preparation time **25 minutes + 3–4 days marinating**
Total cooking time **2 minutes**

Serves 4

300 g (10 oz) goat's cheese (see Chef's tips)
3 sprigs of fresh thyme
1 large sprig of fresh rosemary
15 fresh basil leaves
6 whole black peppercorns, lightly crushed
4 juniper berries, lightly crushed
400 ml (12³/4 fl oz) olive oil
50 g (1³/4 oz) pine nuts
100 g (3¹/4 oz) watercress
100 g (3¹/4 oz) lamb's lettuce

1 Place the goat's cheese on a board and cut off the skin with a sharp knife. Cut into roughly 1 cm (¹/2 inch) cubes and place loosely in a 1-litre preserving jar with an airtight lid, tucking the thyme, rosemary and basil leaves in between the cheese cubes as you go. Drop the crushed peppercorns and juniper berries into the jar and pour in the olive oil. The oil must cover the cheese completely, so add a little more if the shape of your jar requires it. Place in the refrigerator for 3–4 days for the flavours of the herbs to infuse the cheese.

2 Preheat a grill to medium and place the pine nuts on a tray. Grill for 2 minutes, turning several times and taking care not to let the nuts burn. Leave to cool.

3 Separate the watercress out into sprigs. Just before you are ready to serve, place in a bowl with the lamb's lettuce and sprinkle over the pine nuts and the marinated goat's cheese, drizzling about a quarter of the oil over the leaves. Season with salt and plenty of black pepper and serve immediately.

Chef's tips Choose a firm goat's cheese like chèvre for this recipe—soft goat's cheese will break down too much in the oil.

If there is any cheese left over, it will keep for up to a month covered completely in oil and refrigerated. If you are storing it, remove and discard the basil leaves.

Wild rice and haloumi salad

A striking and unusual deep-red wild-rice dish with cubes of white, salty haloumi, fresh mint and beetroot. You could leave out the prosciutto to turn this into a vegetarian dish.

Preparation time **30 minutes**
Total cooking time **1 hour 10 minutes**
Serves **4**

250 g (8 oz) beetroot
185 g (6 oz) brown rice
60 g (2 oz) wild rice
3 tablespoons olive oil
90 g (3 oz) prosciutto
1 onion, finely chopped
rind and juice of 1 small orange
1 tablespoon red wine vinegar
4 spring onions, finely chopped
2 tablespoons fresh parsley, chopped
2 tablespoons fresh mint, chopped
200 g (6¹/₂ oz) haloumi or feta cheese, cubed
fresh mint leaves, to garnish

1 Bring a large pan of salted water to the boil and cook the beetroot in their skins for about 40 minutes, or until tender. Set aside to cool, then peel and finely chop.

2 Meanwhile, bring another large pan of salted water to the boil. Place the brown rice and wild rice together in a sieve and rinse under running water until thoroughly clean. Cook in the simmering water for 20 minutes, or until tender. Drain well.

3 In a small pan, heat a tablespoon of the olive oil and fry the prosciutto for 2 minutes. Remove from the pan, cool and chop finely.

4 In the same pan, heat the remaining olive oil and add the onion and beetroot. Cook gently for 8 minutes, or until the onion is soft, stirring frequently to prevent it sticking. Pour in the orange rind and juice and red wine vinegar, stir and remove from the heat.

5 Place the cooked rice in a bowl with the prosciutto, spring onion, parsley and half the mint. Season generously with salt and black pepper and stir in the beetroot and orange mixture. Transfer to a serving dish and just before serving, sprinkle over the haloumi or feta cheese and the remaining chopped mint. Garnish with the mint leaves.

Kaleidoscope salad

This attractive salad has a bold dressing of fresh ginger, olive oil and coriander and makes an ideal accompaniment to outdoor or grilled food. It can be made up to 12 hours in advance to develop the flavours.

Preparation time **20 minutes**
Total cooking time **25 minutes**
Serves 4–6

2 corn cobs
13 cm (5 inch) length of cucumber
1 small fennel bulb
1/2 red capsicum (pepper)
6 spring onions, finely sliced
4 large ripe tomatoes
105 g (3 1/2 oz) fresh raw shelled peas
2 tablespoons chopped fresh parsley
1 tablespoon chopped fresh coriander
1 tablespoon chopped fresh basil

DRESSING
2.5 cm (1 inch) piece fresh ginger
1 clove garlic, crushed
125 ml (4 fl oz) olive oil
45 ml (1 1/2 fl oz) rice vinegar
1 teaspoon Tabasco sauce
1 teaspoon ground coriander

1 Preheat a grill to hot. Remove the papery husk and fibres from the outside of the corn cobs and place under the grill for about 25 minutes, turning several times, until the corn is mottled brown and tender. Remove from the grill and, when cool enough to handle, place on a board standing upright and cut off the kernels using a downward action with a sharp knife. Place the kernels in a large bowl.

2 Cut the cucumber in half lengthways, remove the seeds with a teaspoon and cut the flesh into dice. Add to the corn. Discard any tough, outer layers of fennel. Remove the seeds, stalk and membrane from the capsicum, then cut this and the fennel into dice. Add to the bowl with the spring onions.

3 Halve two of the tomatoes and remove the seeds with a teaspoon. Cut the flesh into dice and add to the bowl with the peas, parsley, coriander and basil and gently combine everything with a large spoon, taking care not to break up the tomato.

4 To make the dressing, finely grate the ginger and place in a bowl with the garlic. Using the back of a teaspoon, mash to a paste with 1/4 teaspoon salt. Add the olive oil, rice vinegar, Tabasco, ground coriander and season with 1/2 teaspoon salt and 3/4 teaspoon black pepper. Whisk the dressing, pour over the vegetables and toss gently. Slice the remaining tomatoes and arrange around the plates. Place the salad inside the slices to serve.

Lentil and bacon salad

A hearty, warming salad that can be served as a main course or as an accompaniment. The lentils are cooked with the bacon for extra flavour.

Preparation time **30 minutes**
Total cooking time **35 minutes**
Serves 4–6

410 g (13 oz) small green Puy lentils
200 g (6¹/2 oz) piece of smoked bacon
1 small onion, studded with a clove
1 small leek
2 small carrots
2 celery sticks
150 ml (5 fl oz) olive oil
90 ml (3 fl oz) red wine vinegar
1 round lettuce
1 radicchio

1 In a large pan, place the lentils, piece of smoked bacon and the clove-studded onion and cover with a generous amount of water. Bring to the boil and simmer for about 15 minutes, or until the lentils are tender. Remove the pan from the heat and tip the lentils and bacon into a sieve or fine colander to drain, then run under cold water until cold. Leave to drain thoroughly.

2 Slit the green tops of the leek and rinse thoroughly under cold running water to dislodge and remove all traces of dirt or grit. Very finely dice the leek, carrot and celery, then take the bacon out of the lentils and finely dice this also. Discard the clove-studded onion.

3 In a pan, gently fry the bacon until slightly golden and the fat is starting to become crispy. Depending on the amount of oil from the bacon, add 3 tablespoons of the olive oil, the leek, carrot and celery and fry until tender but still a little crisp. Add the lentils to the bacon and vegetables in the pan, season with black pepper and stir over gentle heat for 2 minutes just to warm through (check for saltiness too, you may not need to season with salt if the bacon is quite salty).

4 Mix together the red wine vinegar and the remaining olive oil, then drizzle over the lentil mixture and stir to combine. Arrange the lettuce and radicchio leaves on plates, spoon the warm lentil mixture on top and serve the salad immediately.

Chef's tip Puy lentils do not break up when cooked. If you use ordinary green lentils instead, you may need to reduce the cooking time.

Mixed salad

A deceptively simple, well-dressed salad that is a perfect accompaniment to any meal.

Preparation time **15 minutes**
Total cooking time **Nil**
Serves 4–6

¹/₂ oak leaf lettuce
¹/₂ frisée lettuce
¹/₂ round lettuce
60 g (2 oz) lamb's lettuce
45 g (1¹/₂ oz) mizuna or watercress
20 g (³/₄ oz) fresh coriander

VINAIGRETTE
30 ml (1 fl oz) white wine vinegar
grated rind and juice of 1 lemon
1 teaspoon Dijon mustard
220 ml (7 fl oz) olive oil

1 Tear the lettuce leaves into bite-sized pieces or leave whole, then toss together gently with the herbs in a large salad bowl using your hands.

2 To make the vinaigrette, mix together the vinegar, lemon rind and juice and the mustard in a small bowl. Using a small balloon whisk, gradually whisk in the olive oil. Check the seasoning, adding salt and black pepper as necessary, and drizzle a little of the dressing over the salad leaves. Mix the salad carefully but thoroughly and serve immediately with the remaining vinaigrette on the side.

Lorette salad

A traditional French salad consisting of a colourful combination of lamb's lettuce, celery and beetroot.

Preparation time **15 minutes**
Total cooking time **40 minutes**
Serves 4–6

2 large beetroot
10 small tender celery sticks or 250 g (8 oz) celeriac
220 g (7 oz) lamb's lettuce

VINAIGRETTE
2 tablespoons red wine vinegar
120 ml (4 fl oz) olive oil
dash Worcestershire sauce

1 Bring a pan of salted water to the boil and cook the beetroot in their skins for about 40 minutes, or until tender. Set aside to cool, then peel.

2 To make the vinaigrette, place the vinegar, oil, Worcestershire sauce and a generous seasoning of salt and black pepper into a small bowl. Whisk with a small balloon whisk until incorporated, and set aside.

3 Peel the celery sticks, if necessary, with a vegetable peeler and cut into 0.5 x 4 cm (¹/₄ x 1¹/₂ inch) batons. Cut the beetroot into similar-sized batons and put into a bowl with the celery and lamb's lettuce. Drizzle with the vinaigrette, mix gently to coat, and serve within 1 hour.

Mixed salad (top) and Lorette salad

Smoked trout salad with horseradish sauce

These elegant starters or light meals are topped with a spoonful of trout mousse and served with melba toasts. The trout mousse and horseradish sauce can be made a day in advance and chilled until needed.

Preparation time **30 minutes + 2 hours chilling**
Total cooking time **10 minutes**
Serves 4

220 g (7 oz) smoked trout fillet, skinned
220 g (7 oz) cream cheese
1 cucumber
125 g (4 oz) seedless green grapes
2 large ripe tomatoes
4 slices white bread
100 g (3¹/4 oz) baby spinach
50 g (1³/4 oz) rocket

HORSERADISH SAUCE
30 g (1 oz) horseradish cream
juice of ¹/2 lemon
150 ml (5 fl oz) cream, for whipping

1 Place the trout and cream cheese in a food processor with some salt and black pepper and blend until a smooth purée has formed, scraping down the sides of the bowl several times to ensure it combines evenly.

2 Cut the cucumber in half and peel one half, then remove the seeds with a small teaspoon and dice the flesh of the peeled cucumber very finely. Cut the grapes into quarters. Mix the grapes and cucumber with the trout purée, cover with plastic wrap and chill for about 1–2 hours. Slice the remaining cucumber.

3 Bring a small pan of water to the boil. With the point of a small sharp knife, score a small cross in the skin at the base of the tomatoes. Drop the tomatoes into the boiling water for 10 seconds, then plunge into a bowl of cold water. Peel the skin away from the cross, then cut around and remove the stalk from the tomatoes. Cut the tomatoes in half and cut out the seeds. Dice the flesh into neat squares.

4 Make melba toasts by preheating a grill to medium and toasting the bread on both sides until golden. Using a sharp serrated knife, trim the crusts from the toast and slice each piece of bread in half horizontally. Remove any loose crumbs from the untoasted sides, cut into sixteen triangles and toast the untoasted sides under the grill so the triangles are brown all over.

5 To make the horseradish sauce, place the horseradish cream, lemon juice, cream and some salt and black pepper in a bowl. Using a balloon whisk or electric beaters, whip lightly until thick.

6 Toss the baby spinach, rocket, tomato and sliced cucumber together and divide between four plates. Place a spoonful of the mousse on top of each salad and serve with the melba toast and horseradish sauce.

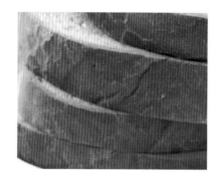

Mixed beans in sweet and sour tomato

A delicious medley of fresh green beans and pulses in a piquant tomato dressing. This salad can be served warm or cold and is ideal as a light lunch with some bread and cheese.

*Preparation time **25 minutes***
*Total cooking time **25 minutes***
Serves 4

375 g (12 oz) fine French beans, trimmed
250 g (8 oz) ripe tomatoes
150 g (5 oz) canned chickpeas
150 g (5 oz) canned red kidney beans
120 ml (4 fl oz) olive oil
2 French shallots, finely chopped
2 teaspoons dark brown sugar
1 clove garlic, crushed
3 tablespoons white wine vinegar
2 red chillies, seeded and finely chopped
15 g (¹/₂ oz) fresh coriander, chopped
15 g (¹/₂ oz) fresh parsley, chopped

1 Bring a pan of salted water to the boil and cook the French beans for 5 minutes, or until just tender but still a little crisp. With the point of a small sharp knife, score a small cross in the skin at the base of the tomatoes, place in a bowl and drain the beans into a colander over them so that the bowl catches the hot water. Set the tomatoes aside while you run cold water over the beans and set them aside to drain thoroughly.

2 Remove the tomatoes from the hot water with a slotted spoon and peel the skin away from the cross, then cut around and remove the stalk from the tomatoes. Slice the tomatoes into quarters, remove and discard the seeds and finely dice the flesh. Rinse the chickpeas and red kidney beans under cold running water and leave these to drain.

3 In a large, heavy-based frying pan, heat 2 tablespoons of the olive oil and cook the shallots over medium heat until they have softened, then stir in the brown sugar, garlic, white wine vinegar and red chillies and continue to cook, stirring, for 3–4 minutes, or until the sugar is beginning to caramelize. Add the diced tomato, season with some salt and black pepper and cover the pan. Lower the heat and simmer for about 10 minutes, stirring once or twice.

4 Gently mix all of the drained beans together in a large bowl with all but 1 tablespoon of the chopped herbs, and season with salt and black pepper. Add the sweet and sour tomato mixture and the remaining olive oil to the bowl, stir gently to combine and sprinkle with the remaining herbs. Serve warm or cold.

Waldorf salad

Traditionally made of apple, celery, walnuts and mayonnaise and created in New York's Waldorf Astoria Hotel in the 1890s, this version is based around the same key ingredients with some added Parma ham.

Preparation time **30 minutes**
Total cooking time **5 minutes**
Serves **6–8**

2 celery hearts
60 g (2 oz) walnut halves
1/2 lemon
4 dessert apples
1 French shallot, very finely chopped
1 clove garlic, very finely chopped
1 tablespoon vegetable oil, for frying
6 slices Parma ham or prosciutto
1 cos or romaine lettuce

DRESSING
2 teaspoons Dijon mustard
4 tablespoons olive oil
4 tablespoons thick (double) cream

1 Using a large sharp knife, cut the celery hearts into thin slices, wash well and set aside to drain thoroughly.
2 Preheat the grill to medium. Spread the walnuts out on the baking tray and grill for 1–2 minutes, or until brown, taking care that they don't burn.

3 Grate the rind of the lemon finely into a large bowl and squeeze in all but a tablespoon of the juice. One at a time, peel, quarter and slice the apples across and toss them gently into the lemon in the bowl to stop them going brown. Add the shallot and garlic with the walnuts, drained celery and a little salt and black pepper.

4 To make the dressing, place the remaining tablespoon of lemon juice in a small bowl and mix with the mustard. Using a small balloon whisk, beat in the olive oil a few drops at a time until the dressing is smooth and emulsified, then beat in the cream for a few seconds until combined. Taste the dressing and season with salt and black pepper.

5 Heat the vegetable oil in a heavy-based, non-stick frying pan and fry the Parma ham for 30 seconds, or until shrivelled slightly. Drain on paper towels, then cut into small strips using scissors or a sharp knife and leave until cool and crispy.

6 Slice the lettuce leaves very thinly and use to line a serving bowl. Drizzle the dressing over the apple and celery, stir gently to mix and toss together with the lettuce. Sprinkle the strips of Parma ham over the salad just before serving.

Salmon salade niçoise

This typical Provençal salad from Nice is traditionally made with tuna, but here it is served with a fillet of salmon. Perfect for a light summer supper.

*Preparation time **20 minutes***
*Total cooking time **1 hour***
Serves 4

310 g (10 oz) small salad potatoes
250 g (8 oz) green beans
8 quail eggs
1 green capsicum (pepper), cut into matchsticks
1 red capsicum (pepper), cut into matchsticks
2 French shallots, finely sliced
4 ripe tomatoes, cut into sixths
4 x 155 g (5 oz) salmon fillets, skinned
1 small round lettuce
100 g (3¼ oz) rocket
20 black olives

VINAIGRETTE
2 tablespoons balsamic vinegar
100 ml (3¼ fl oz) olive oil

1 Bring a large pan of salted water to the boil and add the potatoes in their skins. Return to the boil and simmer for 30–35 minutes, or until they are tender to the point of a knife. Drain, then plunge the potatoes into a bowl of iced water for 5 minutes to stop the cooking process. Drain again and cut in quarters.

2 Bring a large pan of fresh salted water to the boil and trim the ends off the beans. Put in the pan and boil for 8 minutes, or until tender, then place into iced water as above to stop the cooking process and retain the colour of the beans. Drain well.

3 Bring a small pan of salted water to the boil and boil the quail eggs for about 4 minutes, or until hard-boiled. When cooked, run the eggs under cold water, set aside to cool, then shell and halve.

4 To make the vinaigrette, place the balsamic vinegar into a small bowl and whisk in the olive oil and some salt and black pepper with a small balloon whisk. Place the potato quarters, green beans, capsicum, shallots and tomato into a large bowl and toss very gently with half the vinaigrette.

5 Heat a lightly oiled chargrill pan or frying pan over high heat and when hot, place the salmon fillets on and cook for about 10 minutes, or until cooked through, turning once. Remove from the pan and keep warm. Place the lettuce and rocket leaves on four plates and arrange the potato mixture, quail eggs and olives on top. Place a portion of salmon on top of each salad and drizzle with the remaining vinaigrette.

Oriental lime chicken salad

An eastern-flavoured main-course salad with sesame-covered chicken strips topped with caramelized carrot and coriander. Serve with the ginger and lime dressing and extra lime wedges.

*Preparation time **30 minutes***
*Total cooking time **25 minutes***
Serves 4

200 g (6¹/2 oz) skinless chicken breast fillet
2 tablespoons sesame oil
2 tablespoons rice wine or dry sherry
2 tablespoons lime juice
I stalk lemon grass, finely chopped
15 g (¹/2 oz) fresh ginger, grated
I clove garlic, crushed
I red chilli, finely chopped
3 carrots, cut into matchsticks
I tablespoon honey
60 g (2 oz) seasoned flour
I egg, lightly beaten
120 g (4 oz) sesame seeds
vegetable oil, for deep frying
I baby cos lettuce
2 tablespoons fresh coriander, chopped
lime wedges, to serve

DRESSING
I clove garlic, crushed
15 g (¹/2 oz) fresh ginger, grated
2 tablespoons light soy sauce
grated rind and juice of I lime
2 tablespoons sesame oil
I tablespoon rice wine or dry sherry
pinch of sugar

1 Cut the chicken into thin strips and place in a small bowl with the sesame oil, rice wine or dry sherry, lime juice, lemon grass, ginger, garlic and chilli. Stir to coat the chicken thoroughly, cover with plastic wrap and place in the refrigerator.

2 To make the dressing, place all the ingredients in a small bowl and whisk until well combined. Cover and set aside.

3 Place the carrot matchsticks in a small pan with a pinch of salt and just enough boiling water to cover. Add the honey and simmer for about 6–8 minutes, or until the water has evaporated and the carrots are cooked and lightly caramelized. Drain off any excess moisture on paper towels and leave to cool.

4 Remove the chicken from the marinade and drain on paper towels. Place the seasoned flour, the beaten egg and the sesame seeds in three separate bowls. Preheat the oil in a deep-fat fryer or deep saucepan to 180°C (350°F). Place a bread cube in the oil: if it sizzles and turns golden brown in 15 seconds, the oil is hot enough. Toss small batches of the chicken strips in the flour, then in the egg, then in the sesame seeds. Deep-fry the coated chicken strips in two batches for about 8 minutes, or until light golden in colour and cooked through. Drain the chicken on paper towels.

5 Toss the lettuce leaves in half the dressing, then arrange on a serving plate. Place the chicken strips on the lettuce with the caramelized carrot and the coriander sprinkled over the top. Serve the remaining dressing in a separate bowl and pass around the extra lime wedges to serve.

Classic potato salad

A classic potato salad made with freshly prepared mayonnaise.

Preparation time **10 minutes**
Total cooking time **25 minutes**
Serves 4

2 kg (4 lb) waxy potatoes, peeled and cut into cubes
4 tablespoons snipped fresh chives

MAYONNAISE
2 egg yolks
I heaped tablespoon Dijon mustard
   or I heaped teaspoon dried mustard powder
275 ml (9 fl oz) lightly flavoured vegetable oil
I tablespoon white wine vinegar

1 Bring a pan of salted water to the boil. Add the potatoes and boil for 20–25 minutes, or until tender to the point of a knife. Drain well and place in a bowl.
2 To make the mayonnaise, bring all the ingredients to room temperature and set a large bowl on a damp tea towel to prevent it from moving. Add the egg yolks, mustard and a pinch of salt to the bowl and mix with a balloon whisk or electric beaters.
3 Put the oil in a jug that is easy to pour from. While whisking constantly by hand or with electric beaters, pour a steady thin stream of oil into the mixture. Begin with a small amount and stop pouring periodically to allow each addition to emulsify to a thick creamy mixture. Continue until 100 ml (3¹/4 fl oz) of the oil has been added and the mayonnaise has begun to thicken.
4 Add the vinegar to make the texture slightly thinner. Continue gradually adding the oil and adjust the flavour by adding more vinegar, salt and pepper if necessary. Add 1–2 tablespoons of boiling water if it curdles or separates. Stir most of the chives and the mayonnaise into the potatoes until evenly coated and sprinkle the remaining chives over the top.

Mustard seed potato salad

A flavourful potato salad made with whole small potatoes and a mustard mayonnaise.

Preparation time **10 minutes**
Total cooking time **35 minutes**
Serves 4

2 kg (4 lb) small salad or new potatoes, scrubbed

MAYONNAISE
2 egg yolks
275 ml (9 fl oz) lightly flavoured vegetable oil
I tablespoon white wine vinegar
2 heaped tablespoons wholegrain mustard

1 Bring a pan of salted water to the boil. Add the potatoes and boil for 30–35 minutes, or until tender to the point of a knife. Drain well and place in a bowl.
2 To make the mayonnaise, bring all the ingredients to room temperature and set a large bowl on a damp tea towel to prevent it from moving. Add the egg yolks and a pinch of salt to the bowl and mix with a balloon whisk or electric beaters.
3 Put the oil in a jug that is easy to pour from. While whisking constantly by hand or with electric beaters, pour a steady thin stream of oil into the mixture. Begin with a small amount and stop pouring periodically to allow each addition to emulsify to a thick creamy mixture. Continue until 100 ml (3¹/4 fl oz) of the oil has been added and the mayonnaise has begun to thicken.
4 Add the vinegar to make the texture slightly thinner. Continue gradually adding the oil, then stir in the wholegrain mustard. Adjust the flavour by adding more vinegar, salt and pepper if necessary. Add 1–2 tablespoons of boiling water if it curdles or separates. Add the mayonnaise to the potatoes and stir until evenly coated. Serve warm.

Classic potato salad (bottom) and Mustard seed potato salad

Celeriac remoulade

This French classic makes a delicious first course or light lunch. A mustardy mayonnaise enhances the crunchy celeriac's flavour, along with some gherkins, capers and anchovies.

*Preparation time **35 minutes + 1 hour standing***
*Total cooking time **Nil***
Serves 4–6

1.25 kg (2¹/₂ lb) celeriac
juice of 1 lemon
2 ripe tomatoes
2 tablespoons capers
8 gherkins, finely chopped
30 g (1 oz) fresh herbs, such as chervil, basil and dill
105 g (3¹/₂ oz) small salad leaves
8 anchovy fillets, to garnish

REMOULADE SAUCE
2 egg yolks
2 heaped tablespoons Dijon mustard or
** 1 heaped teaspoon dried mustard powder**
pinch of cayenne pepper
275 ml (9 fl oz) lightly flavoured vegetable oil

1 Cut the celeriac in half and peel away the skin, cutting 3 mm (¹/₈ inch) deep into the flesh to remove all of the fibrous skin. Coarsely grate the celeriac, season with salt and black pepper and toss in the lemon juice. Cover with plastic wrap and set aside for 30–60 minutes.

2 To make the remoulade sauce, bring all the ingredients to room temperature and set a large bowl on a damp tea towel to prevent it from moving. Add the egg yolks, mustard, cayenne pepper and a pinch of salt to the bowl and mix with a balloon whisk or electric beaters.

3 Put the oil in a jug that is easy to pour from. While whisking constantly by hand or with electric beaters, pour a steady thin stream of oil into the mixture. Begin with a small amount and stop pouring periodically to allow each addition to emulsify to a thick creamy mixture. Continue until the sauce resembles whipped cream. Add 1–2 tablespoons of boiling water if it curdles or separates.

4 Bring a small pan of water to the boil. With the point of a small sharp knife, score a small cross in the skin at the base of the tomatoes. Drop the tomatoes into the boiling water for 10 seconds, then plunge into a bowl of cold water. Peel the skin away from the cross, then cut around and remove the stalk from the tomatoes. Slice the tomatoes into quarters, remove and discard the seeds and finely dice the flesh. Place in a bowl.

5 Squeeze out the excess liquid from the celeriac and mix with the remoulade sauce. Rinse the capers, dry and chop if they are large, then stir these and the gherkins into the celeriac. Serve decorated with the tomato, herbs and salad leaves, then top with the anchovy fillets.

Melon and seafood sesame salad

A light and elegant main course with fresh flavours and a nutty texture from the sesame dressing.
The seafood can be varied to use whatever is freshest and available.

Preparation time **25 minutes**
Total cooking time **5 minutes**
Serves 4

375 g (12 oz) mussels
165 g (5¹/₂ oz) peeled cooked prawns or shrimps
2 small honeydew or galia melons
185 g (6 oz) white crab meat, drained well if frozen
fresh chervil or mint sprigs, to garnish

DRESSING
2 tablespoons sesame seeds
30 ml (1 fl oz) white wine vinegar
125 ml (4 fl oz) lightly flavoured vegetable oil
2 teaspoons sesame oil

1 Clean the mussels by scrubbing the shells with a brush to remove any sand. Scrape the barnacles off with a knife. Pull off any beards from the mussels. Discard any mussels that are broken, are not tightly closed or do not close when lightly tapped on a work surface.
2 Put the mussels in a large saucepan, sprinkle with water and cook for about 3 minutes over low heat, shaking the pan occasionally, until the mussels open.

Discard any mussels that do not open. Devein the prawns.
3 Cut the melons in half and remove the seeds with a teaspoon. Using a sharp knife, slice into crescents about 1 cm (1/2 inch) thick and peel each crescent.
4 To make the dressing, dry-fry the sesame seeds in a frying pan for 2 minutes, then set aside to cool. Pour the white wine vinegar into a bowl with a little salt and black pepper. Whisk with a small balloon whisk to dissolve the salt, then slowly add the vegetable and sesame oils in a steady, thin stream until the dressing is smooth and thick. Add the sesame seeds and season if necessary with salt and black pepper.
5 Set aside half the mussels for decoration and remove the rest from their shells, placing in a bowl with the prawns and crab meat. Pour enough of the dressing over the seafood to moisten, season well with salt and black pepper and lightly toss to combine. Lay three pieces of melon on four plates and pile the seafood mixture beside them. Arrange the reserved mussels in their shells around the edge of the plates and garnish with sprigs of chervil or mint. Drizzle any remaining dressing over the mussels and serve immediately.

Chef's tip Instead of cooking fresh mussels, you could buy precooked mussels.

Tabouleh

A grain salad that originated in the Lebanon and is made with generous amounts of fresh mint, parsley and bulgar wheat.

Preparation time **20 minutes + 30 minutes soaking**
Total cooking time **Nil**
Serves 4

250 g (8 oz) bulgar wheat
I telegraph cucumber
30 g (I oz) fresh mint, finely chopped
40 g (I1/4 oz) fresh flat-leaf parsley, finely chopped
6 spring onions, finely chopped
90 ml (3 fl oz) olive oil
100 ml (31/4 fl oz) lemon juice
cos or romaine lettuce leaves, to serve

1 Place the bulgar wheat in a bowl and pour in enough hot water to just cover the wheat. Leave to soak for 20–30 minutes. Peel the cucumber and cut in half lengthways. Using a teaspoon, remove the seeds from the centre, then finely dice the flesh. Place the cucumber, mint, parsley and spring onion in a medium bowl with the olive oil and lemon juice.

2 Tip the bulgar wheat into a sieve to drain off any excess water. Fluff up the grains with a fork, add to the bowl with the herbs and season generously with salt and black pepper.

3 Serve with a pile of lettuce leaves. To eat, place some tabouleh in the centre of each lettuce leaf and fold into a parcel.

Rustic Greek salad

A hearty salad with the Greek flavours of feta, oregano, black olives and ripe tomatoes.

Preparation time **15 minutes**
Total cooking time **Nil**
Serves 4

I romaine or cos lettuce
3 ripe tomatoes
125 g (4 oz) Kalamata olives
I French shallot, finely chopped
250 g (8 oz) feta cheese
I tablespoon fresh oregano leaves, chopped
60 ml (2 fl oz) olive oil
60 ml (2 fl oz) lemon juice

1 Shred the romaine or cos lettuce finely and place on plates. Cut the tomatoes into slim wedges and arrange over the lettuce with the olives and shallot.

2 Cut the fetta cheese into 2 cm (3/4 inch) cubes and scatter these over the salad with the oregano. Season with salt and black pepper.

3 Whisk together the oil and lemon juice and pour it over the salads.

Seared scallop and mango salsa salad

A very pretty starter for a special occasion. The scallops and salsa can be prepared ahead, leaving just the brief cooking of the scallops to the last minute.

*Preparation time **30 minutes***
*Total cooking time **5 minutes***
Serves 4

16 large scallops
1 tablespoon olive oil
15 g (¹/₂ oz) unsalted butter
baby salad leaves, to serve
a few sprigs of fresh coriander, to garnish

MANGO SALSA
6 ripe tomatoes
2 ripe mangoes
15 g (¹/₂ oz) fresh coriander leaves, finely chopped
2 large French shallots, finely chopped
2 green chillies, finely chopped
juice of 2 limes

1 If the scallops are in their shells, remove them by sliding a knife underneath the white muscle and orange roe. Wash the scallops to remove any grit or sand, then pull away the small tough shiny muscle and the black vein, leaving the orange roe intact. Dry the scallops on paper towels, cover and chill.

2 To make the mango salsa, bring a small pan of water to the boil. With the point of a small sharp knife, score a small cross in the skin at the base of the tomatoes. Drop the tomatoes in the boiling water for 10 seconds, then plunge into a bowl of cold water. Peel the skin away from the cross, then cut around and remove the stalk from the tomatoes. Slice the tomatoes into quarters, remove and discard the seeds and dice the flesh into 1 cm (¹/₂ inch) cubes.

3 Dice the mangoes into similar sized pieces as the tomato and mix with the tomato, coriander leaves, shallots, chilli and lime juice and season with salt and black pepper. Cover and chill until ready to serve.

4 Heat the olive oil in a non-stick frying pan, add the butter and when it has melted and starts foaming, place the scallops in the pan. Cook for about 3–4 minutes, or until lightly golden on both sides and just tender to the touch. Arrange a bed of baby salad leaves on four plates and spoon over the mango salsa. Top with the warm scallops, any juices and the coriander sprigs and serve the salad immediately.

Smoked chicken salad with macadamia nut dressing

This delicious salad contains all the ingredients for a wonderful lunch or light supper—smoked chicken and asparagus with peppery rocket and French baguette slices.

Preparation time **20 minutes**
Total cooking time **15 minutes**
Serves 4

185 g (6 oz) asparagus
12 thin slices French baguette
150 g (5 oz) rocket leaves
2 smoked chicken breasts, about 180 g (5³/4 oz) each
a few sprigs of fresh chervil, to garnish

DRESSING
60 g (2 oz) macadamia nuts
3 tablespoons white wine vinegar
2 tablespoons olive oil
3 tablespoons macadamia or hazelnut oil

1 Bring a large pan of salted water to the boil. Use a vegetable peeler to remove the outer layer from the lower two thirds of the stem of each asparagus spear, then snap the woody ends off at their natural breaking point and discard. Cut the spears into 2.5 cm (1 inch) lengths and add to the water. Reduce the heat and simmer until the tips are tender. Remove and run under cold water, then drain on paper towels.

2 To make the dressing, preheat the grill to medium. Place the macadamia nuts onto a baking tray and grill for 5 minutes, taking care not to let them burn. Cool slightly before chopping with a sharp knife.

3 Place the slices of baguette on a tray in a single layer and toast for about 5 minutes on each side under the grill, or until crisp and golden brown.

4 Place the vinegar, olive oil and macadamia or hazelnut oil into a small bowl and whisk using a small balloon whisk until they are combined, then stir in the chopped macadamia nuts and season well with salt and black pepper.

5 Place the rocket in a large bowl. Give the dressing a stir to distribute the nuts and drizzle a little over the leaves, tossing to thoroughly coat. Arrange the baguette slices and rocket on four plates.

6 Cut the smoked chicken into bite-sized pieces. Place the chicken and asparagus in a small bowl, stir the dressing and pour over a little to coat. Place the chicken and asparagus on the rocket and top with the chervil.

Chef's tip If making the dressing in advance, add the nuts just before using.

Warm fennel and cherry tomato salad

The dressing for this salad is an aromatic herb oil, made a week in advance to allow the flavours to infuse. If making extra, the oil keeps well and is perfect for drizzling over grilled meat and fish.

*Preparation time **10 minutes + 1 week infusing***
*Total cooking time **30 minutes***
Serves 4

AROMATIC OIL
50 ml (1³/4 fl oz) sesame oil
250 ml (8 fl oz) olive oil
100 ml (3¹/4 fl oz) hazelnut oil
1 bay leaf
1 sprig of fresh thyme
1 sprig of fresh rosemary

3 large or 4 small fennel bulbs with frondy green tops
1 sprig of fresh thyme
375 g (12 oz) ripe cherry or baby plum tomatoes
45 g (1¹/2 oz) Pecorino or Parmesan cheese,
  freshly shaved

1 Begin by making the aromatic oil at least one week in advance. Place the oils, bay leaf, thyme and rosemary in a pan and heat gently for 5 minutes, without boiling. Season well. Cool, then transfer to a sterilized screwtop bottle or jar and store the oil in the refrigerator for a week, turning the bottle occasionally. After a week, decant the oil into a clean bottle, discarding the herbs.

2 To make the salad, trim the fronds from the top of the fennel bulbs and reserve for garnish, then cut the fennel into eighths, leaving a little of the base on each section to hold it together. Brush generously with about 75 ml (2¹/2 fl oz) of the aromatic oil.

3 Heat a chargrill pan until it is very hot and brush with a little of the oil. Alternatively, the vegetables can be placed under a preheated grill, but then they will not have the attractive charred lines. Place the fennel on the pan and cook for about 10 minutes each side, or until tender, caramelized and lightly charred. When the fennel is cooked, set aside and keep warm.

4 Heat the remaining oil in a large shallow pan until very hot. Carefully place the thyme and tomatoes in the hot oil and fry for 2–3 minutes, or until the skins are just splitting. Remove with a slotted spoon, discarding the thyme and reserving the oil, and pile up on a plate with the fennel and any juices. Top with the Pecorino or Parmesan and reserved fennel fronds. Season with some salt and black pepper and drizzle over some of the oil from cooking the tomatoes. Serve immediately with fresh bread.

Thai pork salad

This cold Thai salad is a whole meal by itself. The pork is marinated in coconut, chilli, lime juice, lemon grass and fresh coriander, quickly stir-fried, then tossed with rice noodles.

*Preparation time **40 minutes + 4 hours marinating***
*Total cooking time **15 minutes***
Serves 4

90 g (3 oz) fresh coconut
300 g (10 oz) pork fillet (tenderloin)
30 g (1 oz) fresh coriander leaves
2 green chillies, seeded and chopped
2 tender stalks lemon grass, finely chopped
juice of 3 limes
3 tablespoons soy sauce
3 tablespoons sesame oil
3 teaspoons light brown sugar
220 g (7 oz) mangetout
250 g (8 oz) rice vermicelli, rice stick or
  cellophane noodles
1 tablespoon vegetable oil
225 g (7¹/4 oz) tin water chestnuts, sliced
1 tablespoon sesame seeds

1 Preheat the grill to hot. Pare four strips off the coconut using a potato peeler and grate the rest. Place the strips of coconut under the grill for 3 minutes, or until tinged brown along the edges, then set these aside.
2 Prepare the pork by trimming off any fat and sinew and cutting with a sharp knife into thin strips 6 cm (2¹/2 inches) long. Reserve a few coriander leaves for a garnish, then chop the remainder and place into a bowl with the chilli, lemon grass, half the lime juice and half the grated coconut. Add the pork strips, stir to combine, then cover and marinate in the refrigerator for at least 30 minutes and up to 4 hours.
3 In a small bowl, mix together the remaining grated coconut and lime juice, the soy sauce, 1 tablespoon of the sesame oil and the brown sugar and set aside. Trim the ends off the mangetout. Place the rice or cellophane noodles in a bowl, pour over 1 litre of boiling water and set aside.
4 Heat the vegetable oil in a wok or heavy-based frying pan until hot and add the pork with its marinade, the water chestnuts and the soy sauce mixture (stand back a little from the stove as it may spit). Toss the pork around in the wok with a long-handled spoon or tongs for 5 minutes, or until cooked through, then remove to a plate. Stir-fry the mangetout in the same wok or pan for 3 minutes, then add to the pork. Drain the noodles well and pour in the remaining sesame oil, the sesame seeds and ¹/2 teaspoon salt.
5 Toss the noodles with the pork and place in a dish. Garnish with the coconut strips and the reserved coriander leaves.

Three-tomato salad

Succulent semi-dried tomatoes made at home are far superior to shop-bought ones and the tomato flavour is wonderfully intense without sacrificing any texture.

Preparation time 15 minutes + 1 day marinating
Total cooking time 2 hours
Serves 4

SEMI-DRIED TOMATOES
1 kg (2 lb) ripe plum (Roma) tomatoes
sea salt
2 tablespoons fresh thyme leaves
1 tablespoon fresh marjoram leaves
300 ml (10 fl oz) olive oil

4 large ripe red tomatoes
250 g (8 oz) yellow cherry tomatoes
2 tablespoons balsamic vinegar
2 tablespoons snipped fresh chives

1 At least one day before you wish to serve the salad, preheat the oven to warm 160°C (315°F/Gas 2–3). Halve the plum tomatoes and scoop out the seeds. Place the tomatoes, cut-side uppermost, on baking trays.

Sprinkle sparingly with some sea salt, black pepper and the thyme and marjoram, making sure that each tomato half gets some. Place the trays of tomato halves in the oven for about 1 hour 45 minutes to 2 hours, or until the tomatoes are puckered and shrunken but still moist. Place them in a clean preserving jar and add enough olive oil to cover completely. Refrigerate until needed.

2 Slice the red tomatoes thinly and arrange in overlapping circles on a serving plate. Cut the cherry tomatoes in half and arrange with the oven-dried tomatoes inside the red ones. Season well with salt and black pepper and drizzle over three tablespoons of the semi-dried tomato oil, the balsamic vinegar and the snipped chives.

Chef's tips If you do not want to use all the semi-dried tomatoes in this salad, they will keep for up to two weeks covered in their oil in the refrigerator.

If you can find large yellow tomatoes, you can buy these instead of the red ones, then use red cherry tomatoes instead of the yellow.

Duck salad with plum dressing

*This easy and unusual salad has a wonderful flavour and is glamorous enough for
a dinner party starter.*

Preparation time **20 minutes**
Total cooking time **10 minutes**
Serves 4

DRESSING
1 x 250 g (8 oz) tinned plums in syrup, stoned
1 tablespoon honey
1 teaspoon Worcestershire sauce
1 tablespoon dark soy sauce
1/2 teaspoon Tabasco sauce

4 x 220 g (7 oz) duck breasts
4 slices white bread
60 g (2 oz) unsalted butter
1 tablespoon olive oil
2 cloves garlic, crushed
4 spring onions
185 g (6 oz) curly endive

1 To make the dressing, place the plums and their syrup, the honey, Worcestershire, soy and Tabasco sauces in a small pan. Bring to the boil over medium heat and simmer for 5 minutes, then remove from the heat and allow to cool. Once cooled, place the plum mixture with all the liquid into a blender or food processor and process until completely smooth. Check the seasoning, adding salt and black pepper only if necessary, and transfer to a small bowl. Cover and chill.

2 Prick the duck breasts all over with a fork and place them, skin-side-down, in a hot frying pan. Cook for about 5 minutes, or until the skin is well-browned and the fat melted out. Turn them over and cook the other side for about 2 minutes, or until cooked through.

3 Remove the crusts from the bread and cut the bread into 2 cm (3/4 inch) cubes. In a large heavy-based frying pan, heat the butter, oil and garlic over medium heat until the butter has melted, raise the heat a little, then add the cubes of bread and cook for 2–3 minutes, stirring frequently to ensure they cook to an even golden colour without burning. Remove the pan from the heat, drain the croutons on crumpled paper towels and sprinkle with a little salt and black pepper.

4 Remove the skin from the duck breasts if you prefer and slice across into 5 mm (1/4 inch) thick slices. Slice the spring onions diagonally and tear the curly endive into bite-sized pieces. Toss the spring onion, endive and half the croutons in about 1 tablespoon of the plum dressing just to coat and pile into a dish. Arrange the duck slices on top and scatter over the remaining croutons. Serve immediately with the remaining plum sauce offered separately.

Published in 2000 by Merehurst Limited, Ferry House, 51–57 Lacy Road, Putney, London SW15 1PR.

Murdoch Books and Le Cordon Bleu would like to express their gratitude to the 42 masterchefs of all the Le Cordon Bleu Schools, whose knowledge and expertise have made this book possible, especially: Chef Terrien, Chef Boucheret, Chef Deguignet, Chef Duchêne (MOF), Chef Guillut, Chef Pinaud, Chef Cros, Paris; Chef Males, Chef Walsh, Chef Power, Chef Carr, Chef Paton, Chef Poole-Gleed, Chef Wavrin, Chef Thivet, London; Chef Chantefort, Chef Jambert, Chef Hamasaki, Chef Honda, Chef Paucod, Chef Okuda, Chef Lederf, Chef Peugeot, Chef Mori, Tokyo; Chef Salambien, Chef Boutin, Chef Harris, Sydney; Chef Lawes, Adelaide; Chef Guiet, Chef Denis, Chef Petibon, Chef Poncet, Ottawa; Chef Martin, Mexico; Chef Camargo, Brazil.
A very special acknowledgment to Helen Barnard, Alison Oakervee and Deepika Sukhwani, who have been responsible for the coordination of the Le Cordon Bleu team throughout this series under the Presidency of André J Cointreau.

Series Manager: Kay Halsey
Series Concept, Design and Art Direction: Juliet Cohen
Food Editor: Lulu Grimes
Designer: Wing Ping Tong
Photographer: André Martin
Food Stylist: Carolyn Fienberg
Food Preparation: Justine Poole
Home Economist: Michaela Le Compte

Creative Director: Marylouise Brammer
CEO & Publisher: Anne Wilson

ISBN 1 85391 985 3

Printed by Toppan Printing Hong Kong Co. Ltd. PRINTED IN CHINA
First Printed 2000
©Design and photography Murdoch Books® 2000
©Text Le Cordon Bleu 2000

A catalogue record for this book is available from the British Library.

Distributed in the UK by D Services, 6 Euston Street, Freemen's Common, Leicester LE2 7SS Tel 0116-254-7671 Fax 0116-254-4670.
Distributed in Canada by Whitecap (Vancouver) Ltd, 351 Lynn Avenue, North Vancouver, BC V7J 2C4 Tel 604-980-9852 Fax 604-980-8197 or Whitecap (Ontario) Ltd, 47 Coldwater Road, North York, ON M3B 1Y8 Tel 416-444-3442 Fax 416-444-6630
Published and distributed in Australia by Murdoch Books®, GPO Box 1203, Sydney NSW 1045

Front cover: Warm fennel and cherry tomato salad

IMPORTANT INFORMATION

CONVERSION GUIDE

1 cup = 250 ml (8 fl oz)
1 Australian tablespoon = 20 ml (4 teaspoons)
1 UK tablespoon = 15 ml (3 teaspoons)

NOTE: We have used 20 ml tablespoons. If you are using a 15 ml tablespoon, for most recipes the difference will be negligible. For recipes using baking powder, gelatine, bicarbonate of soda and flour, add an extra teaspoon for each tablespoon specified.

CUP CONVERSIONS—DRY INGREDIENTS

1 cup flour, plain or self-raising = 125 g (4 oz)
1 cup sugar, caster = 250 g (8 oz)
1 cup breadcrumbs, dry = 125 g (4 oz)

IMPORTANT: Those who might be at risk from the effects of salmonella food poisoning (the elderly, pregnant women, young children and those suffering from immune deficiency diseases) should consult their GP with any concerns about eating raw eggs.